FREDERICK DOUGLASS

AND THE

NORTH STAR

LORENZO PACE

WINDMILL BOOKS

New York

Published in 2015 by The Rosen Publishing Group, Inc.
29 East 21st Street, New York, NY 10010

First Edition

Book Design: Brian Garvey

Illustrator: Lorenzo Pace

Library of Congress Cataloging-in-Publication Data

Pace, Lorenzo.
Frederick Douglass and the North Star / by Lorenzo Pace.
p. cm. — (African American quartet)
ISBN 978-1-4777-9281-0 (library binding) — ISBN 978-1-4777-9282-7 (pbk.) — ISBN 978-1-4777-9283-4 (6-pack)
1. Douglass, Frederick, 1818–1895 — Juvenile literature. 2. Abolitionists — United States — Juvenile literature. 3. African American abolitionists — Juvenile literature. 4. Antislavery movements — United States — History — 19th century — Juvenile literature. I. Pace, Lorenzo. II. Title.
E449.D75 P334 2015
973.8—d23

Manufactured in the United States of America

All artwork by Lorenzo Pace.
Cover photo SuperStock/Getty Images, p. 47 Cindy Reiman.

FREDERICK DOUGLASS

AND THE NORTH STAR

This book is about slavery and the brave people who fought against it. More than three hundred years ago, some people in Africa were sold into slavery.

Fig. 226. Slave transport in Africa

5

These African slaves traveled to the United States in sailing ships. They were packed in tightly under horrible conditions. Many died during the voyage.

Many people did not believe that one person should own another. These people protested. They were abolitionists. They wanted to abolish slavery.

But slavery continued because many landowners, especially in the Southern states of the United States, made money from others' work. These people needed slaves to work in the fields.

Throughout the Southern states, there were slave markets where people were bought and sold.

13

Some slaves managed to escape to freedom. One heroic former slave who dedicated his life to help free his brothers and sisters was Frederick Douglass.

15

He wrote a book about his life as a slave. Many people read his book and were moved by what he had to say. They, too, wanted to join him to end slavery.

17

Many joined the struggle,
including the former
slave Harriet Tubman.
She worked on the
Underground Railroad,
and helped slaves to
freedom in the North.

The Underground Railroad was a network of secret routes that helped slaves travel to the North and to freedom. Many people risked their lives to help the slaves avoid capture.

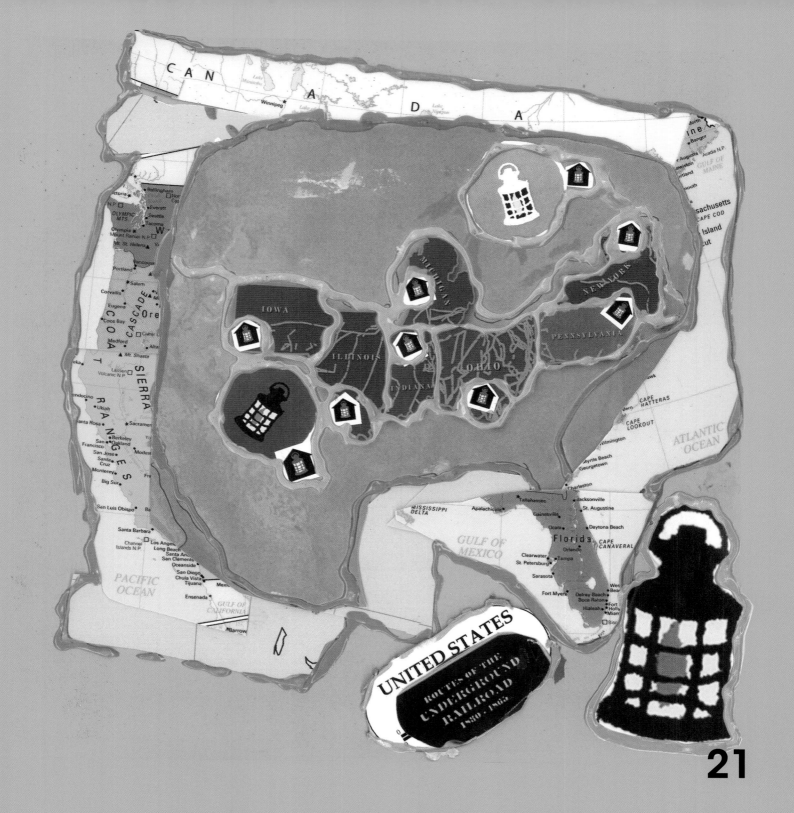

21

William Garrison was never a slave, but he was one of the men who helped with the struggle. He worked with Frederick Douglass to make a newspaper: *The North Star*. This newspaper told people about slavery.

Frederick Douglass wrote for *The North Star*. He was an excellent writer and he convinced many people with his words.

FREDERICK DOUGLASS

"It is easier to build strong children than to repair broken men."

Frederick Douglass not only wrote strongly against slavery, he also spoke in front of many people. He spoke often at the African Church in Rochester, New York, where he lived.

The slave owners fought back. They did not want their slaves to be free. They thought of these people as their property. When a slave escaped, the owners put advertisements in the newspaper and offered rewards.

Frederick Douglass never stopped fighting for justice. His courage was recognized by many people. The president of the United States, Abraham Lincoln, even invited Frederick Douglass to the White House.

31

Abraham Lincoln believed that The United States should be a country that did not have slaves. Many people in the Southern states disagreed. The Northern states and the Southern states fought a civil war because of this disagreement. Many African American soldiers fought for the Northern states. Many died to end slavery. The Northern states won the war. Owning slaves was now against the law.

Frederick Douglass died on February 20, 1895. He lived to see slavery come to an end. His determination, hard work, and persuasive writing helped to make this happen.

FREDERICK DOUGLASS, AMERICAN SLAVE.

"Once you learn to read, you will be forever free."

35

When I was a little boy
in Alabama, each room
of my two-room wooden
schoolhouse had a picture
of Frederick Douglass.
He was a hero to all the
teachers and students. Our
teachers taught us that to
learn to read and write was
our most important job.

Aunt Evelyn

Grandma Mary Wynn Pace

Grandma Laura Clark

EDDIE

DOROTHY

MARY

LORENZO

DAD

MON

ALFONSO

LAWRENCE

Celebrating 65 Years of Marriage...
Mr. and Mrs. Willie Clark, Jr.
April 13, 2013
Still Here.....
On this day many years ago.

Uncle Julius Pace

PraTT
SchooL

FREDERICK DOUGLAS

Grandpa Willie Clark

37

Learning to read was a gift that some people were denied. Frederick Douglass was taught to read by the person who owned him.

"Once you learn to read, you will be forever free."

39

The books that Frederick Douglass wrote made many people think about African Americans differently. Future generations were influenced by his powerful words about dignity and human rights for all people.

41

The leaders of the civil rights movement, such as Martin Luther King Jr., Booker T. Washington, George Washington Carver, and Claudette Colvin, all knew the words of Frederick Douglass. You can say that they were the children of his way of thinking.

16" ST. BAPTIST CHURCH

Emancipation Proclamation

43

I am a child of the thoughts of Frederick Douglass. All my life I collected his books and documents about his life. My sculpture "Triumph of the Human Spirit," in the heart of New York City, celebrates our African American ancestors. *The North Star* showed me the way.

45

Born in Birmingham, Alabama, Lorenzo Pace spent his adolescence in Chicago, Illinois. He received his BFA and MFA degrees from the School of the Art Institute of Chicago and his doctorate in art education and administration from Illinois State University in Normal, Illinois. Working with a diversity of objects and materials, Lorenzo has exhibited his sculpture and installations and presented his performance art both nationally and internationally.

In 1992, he was presented with the Keys to the City of Birmingham, Alabama, by Mayor Richard Arrington and Birmingham councilmen Leroy "Tuffy" Bandy and Bernard Kincaid. In 2000, Lorenzo's work was included in "Out of Action: Performance Art 1949–1999," an exhibition of the Museum of Contemporary Art, Tokyo. In the 2008 Olympics in Beijing, Lorenzo represented the United States in an exhibition entitled "One World One Dream" at the Sunshine International Museum of Contemporary Art.

In 2011, investigating his family roots in Tuskegee, Alabama, Lorenzo included as part of a permanent historical marker and art installation a bronze replica of the original slave lock that had held his great-grandfather captive. This installation is at the AME Zion Church in Creek Stand, Alabama, one of the oldest existing slave cemeteries in the United States.

In 2013, Lorenzo's work was also part of a site-specific art installation to honor those people who were taken as slaves from Buea, Cameroon. This installation was part of the "Festival of Sounds, Color, and Arts of Africa" in Douala, Cameroon.

In 2014, Lorenzo was invited to participate in "HistoryMakers," a video oral history of contemporary artists, writers, musicians, actors, and dancers that is now part of the permanent collection at the Library of Congress in Washington, D.C.

Lorenzo currently maintains a studio in Brooklyn, New York. He is the sculptor commissioned to create "Triumph of the Human Spirit" for the African Burial Ground Memorial in Foley Square Park in New York City. He is currently a professor of art at the University of Texas–Rio Grande Valley.

Acknowledgments

The last twenty-five years of continuous personal research of my family tree has been a daunting task, but the end result was to find my family's roots. These books are a major part of this ongoing search, and they are dedicated to many family members and friends. Starting with members of the Clark family who are present today: to Uncle Willie Clark Jr. (1909), Aunt Evelyn Clark (1929), and Elnora Clark Peewee (1914) in Birmingham, Alabama. To members who have passed in the Pace family: my resolute uncle Julian Pace (1911–2006), who presented the original slave lock to me, and to my mother Mary A. Pace (1916–1993) and father Bishop Elder Eddie T. Pace (1909–1991).

These books are also dedicated to my children: Shawn, Ezra, Jalani (the namesake for the first book), and Esperanza. Much respect and thanks to my cousin Shari Williams, director of the Ridge Project of Tuskegee, Alabama, for taking on the difficult task of researching my family tree, starting in Creek Stand, Alabama, the original place of the slave lock of Steve Pace. To all my friends and colleagues who encouraged me to keep going and not to give up on my quest to better understand our collective humanity.

To my little brother Ronald Pace, who is an author himself (*Cane Is Able*, 2012), for his invaluable suggestions and support, which enabled these books to come alive. To the great artist, printmaker, and musician Jose William, who gave me my first art exhibition at the South Side Art Center in Chicago and helped me make my first silk-screen quilt print. To my old Chicago friend and entrepreneur Walter Patrick, who in 1989 first suggested that the publishers review the prototype for *Jalani and the Lock*. Without this introduction, the book might not have come to fruition.

To my colleague Professor Leila Hernandez, an excellent graphic designer at the University of Texas–Rio Grande Valley, for her suggestion to use my grandmother's and mother's quilts as part of the visual concept of the Harriet Tubman volume. To Chicago impresario and author Tom Burrell (*Brainwashed*, 2004), who believed in me before I believed in myself, praising my early artwork and collecting it to this day. To Cassandra Griffen, photojournalist, for her gracious contribution in allowing me to use her photograph of Birmingham civil rights icon Fred Shuttlesworth.

To my soul mate, former teacher at the School of the Art Institute of Chicago, and author Ronne Hartfield (*Another Way Home*, 2004), who introduced me to African literature and heritage as a young art student. This self-reflection led me to the African symbol "Sankofa" meaning "in order to understand oneself as a person, you must look back at your past to move forward into the future." Therefore, to start this process, I had to go to the Motherland of all humanity, Africa.

All this could not have happened without the help, support, and understanding of one of my dearest friends, Lamine Gueye, and his very special family in Dakar, Senegal, West Africa. My travels there to one of Africa's largest slave castles in Gorée Island have provided me with invaluable information and research on the early slave trade to the Americas.

To the publisher Roger Rosen, who had the courage and vision to tackle some of America's most sensitive topics. His orchestration and sensitivity to the completion of these books have made me keenly aware of what a privilege it was to collaborate with this forward-thinking human being. To Brian Garvey, a wonderful graphic designer who was completely up to the challenge of creatively manipulating the visual concepts of the books. Finally, to my brothers and sisters in the Pace family: Eddie Jr., Lawrence, Michael, Alfonzo, William, Ronald, Dorothy, Mary, Shirley, and my sweet sister-in-law Yvonne. To all our future children and to the visionaries who believe in the essence of humanity, so that we can all live in peace and love, celebrating our differences on this beautiful planet that we all share.

~ Dr. Lorenzo Pace